TRAPPED IN A VIDEO GAME

BOOK ONE

DUSTIN BRADY

CONTENTS

ACKNOWLEDGMENTS

Special thanks to Jesse Brady for the cover and interior illustrations. You can check out more of Jesse's sweet artwork on Instagram: @jessnetic.

CHAPTER ONE
Boogers and Blasters

Jesse. Come over. Now. You're not going to believe this.

That was the text that ruined my life.

I know I know, that doesn't sound like a life ruiner. Especially because the text's sender, my friend Eric, says "you're not going to believe this" about the world's most believable things. Just in the last month, he's told me that I wouldn't believe a piece of toast that looked "exactly like Darth Vader" (it looked exactly like a burnt piece of toast), a sweet trick he learned on his bike (riding for literally one half of one second without holding onto the handlebars) and a really big booger (that one actually was pretty impressive).

I ignored the text for a little bit, because nothing makes Eric talk faster than silence. When he didn't write back after five minutes, I finally replied.

What is it?

No response.

You gonna tell me or what?

Nothing.

This better not be another booger.

Nope.

Five more minutes went by. I sighed. Fine, Eric was going to win this one. But only because looking at his dumb booger would be more fun than this math homework. I closed my book, put on my jacket and walked across the street to Eric's house.

The door was open, so I let myself in and walked down to the basement. "All right, let's see it," I said as I reached the bottom of the stairs.

No booger. Also no Eric.

"Come on," I called out. I wandered into the laundry room (where the dirty clothes should be). I walked upstairs into Eric's room (where the dirty clothes actually were). I checked behind all the doors, inside all the closets and under all the beds. No booger. No Eric.

I couldn't believe it.

Ever since Eric's family moved into the house across the street from mine in first grade, his favorite activity has been playing practical jokes on me. I appreciate a good practical joke as much as the next guy; unfortunately, none of Eric's practical jokes are good. Because he's so impatient, he ruins every joke before it even begins. I don't know how many sleepovers I've been to where Eric has attempted to dip a sleeping friend's finger in warm water, only to have the water dumped over his head by the "victim" who'd had his eyes closed for less than 30 seconds.

So on one hand, I had to admire Eric's commitment to this particular joke. On the other, it may have been his dumbest yet.

Back in the basement, I decided that I'd had enough. "OK!" I yelled to an empty house. "I'm going back home now! I have to finish the math homework due Monday! Maybe you should do the same!"

More silence. I looked around. The only sign of life anywhere was a video game paused on the TV in the corner. Eric loved his video games. Especially the one on the screen right now — *Full Blast*. Never heard of *Full Blast*? That's because it's not out yet. Eric got it two weeks ago from Charlie, the coolest kid in our class. To clarify — Charlie isn't the coolest kid in sixth grade because he's actually a cool kid. He's the coolest because his dad works for a video game company and sometimes gives Charlie's friends early copies of games to test.

For the last two weeks, Eric's mouth has been going full blast about *Full Blast*.

"Jesse, I'm telling you. It is the greatest video game ever made!"

"I don't care."

"All these aliens are trying to take over the world, and you're the only person alive who can save everyone, because…"

"I don't care."

"Because you found one of their blasters, and once you charge it to FULL BLAST you can…"

"I DON'T CARE!"

"You can start shooting…"

Eric never stopped trying to get me to watch him play his new game. I never went because I would rather get sprayed in the face with a fire hose full blast than watch someone else play video games. I don't hate video games — I'm sure they're fine. I've just never really had time to sit down and play them.

I walked toward the TV. I'd never heard Eric rant

about a game like he ranted about this one. Maybe I should give it a chance. At the very least, it would probably beat math homework. I picked up the controller and looked at the screen.

ARE YOU SURE?

- YES

- NO

I paused for a second. Should I? What if I erased Eric's saved game? Nah, he wouldn't mind. He'd just be happy I was trying a video game. I clicked **YES**.

The instant I did everything went black. Not everything on the screen. Everything in *the room*.

CHAPTER TWO
Humanity's Only Hope

You know that feeling you get when you're drinking milk while skydiving and your skydiving buddy tells a funny joke, so you laugh the milk out of your nose and then you throw up at the same time? No? That's not an experience that everyone has? Well anyways, that's exactly how I felt after clicking "YES."

Like I said, everything went black the second I pressed the button. I panicked and felt around for some sort of "undo." One problem — the controller was no longer in my hands. I reached back for the couch. That caused me to lose my balance and start falling into the blackness. As I fell faster, my insides started feeling like they wanted to be outsides, and then I think I barfed, and then I thought, "video games are the worst," and then I blacked out.

When I finally opened my eyes again, I was staring at the sun — which is funny, because if there's one thing that is definitely not in Eric's basement, it's the sun. I felt the ground. Dirt. OK, super weird. I closed my eyes to get my bearings, and then I opened them again to see two angry eyes, two inches away, staring back.

"AHHHHHHHH!"

"NAP TIME'S OVER, MAGGOT!"

The two eyes were attached to a snarling drill sergeant who seemed just like the most furious person ever. I tried backing away.

"Look, I don't... This is a big... OK, listen, if you just call my mom..."

The drill sergeant did not seem interested in clearing things up with Mrs. Rigsby. Instead, he picked me up by the neck just like a bully on TV would.

"Listen maggot, I don't know how you got that blaster attached to your arm, but it's there now, and we're going to use it to..."

The what attached to my what? I looked down. A blaster. Attached to my arm. Where my left hand should be.

"AHHHHHHHHHHH!"

My screaming did nothing to stop the drill sergeant from continuing his little speech.

"...Blast the alien scum back to whatever rock they came from. You are humanity's only hope for..."

"AHHHHHHHHHH!"

"...This planet. Your mission will be long, your mission will be difficult, your mission will probably be deadly. But you..."

"AAAAAAAAAAAAAHHHHHHHHHHHHHHHH HHHHHHHHH!"

I continued screaming through the rest of the speech. After a few more minutes of talking about how I was probably going to die, the sergeant let me go. I sat on the ground, hyperventilating and trying to tear the blaster from my arm.

Over my breathing, I heard the sergeant start talking again. "...to walk around."

I looked up at him. "What was that?"

He stared angrily for a few seconds before repeating himself. "Move the C-stick to walk around."

I blinked a couple of times. "Listen, I don't know what this is supposed to be, but you've got to help me."

He stared back. I took a few steps closer.

"I'm not supposed to be..."

"Good. Now press 'A' to jump."

I squinted at him. "Are you even listening to me?"

He didn't react.

"OK, my name is Jesse Rigsby. I am in the sixth grade. I am not some sort of alien slayer. I don't even believe in aliens, if we're being honest. Can you please just help me get this thing off my arm so I can go home and finish my homework? Please?"

"Press 'A' to jump."

"No! I don't want to jump!"

"Press 'A' to jump."

"This is a video game thing, right? Like virtual reality? Some sort of headset?"

I reached up to tear the headset off. Instead I bonked myself with the very real blaster stuck to my very real arm.

"Press 'A' to jump."

"OK, Eric. Eric Conrad. Hyperactive kid about yay high. He's the one who brought me here. You've seen him, right?"

"Press 'A' to…"

"FINE!" I jumped. "Happy now?"

"Well done. Now it's time to blast some aliens. Follow me."

"No, it is certainly not time to blast some aliens!" I yelled after the drill sergeant. "It's time to get back to math homework! Fractions! I'M SUPPOSED TO BE

MULTIPLYING FRACTIONS!"

As usual, he ignored me. I finally huffed and followed him. What else could I do? He led me through an empty military base, past rows of barracks, to some sort of firing range. He picked up a gun of his own, opened a gate for me and led me into a stall. Ten yards in front of me stood a cardboard cutout of a man-sized praying mantis.

"This is where you'll learn how to use your blaster."

"I very much don't want to use my blaster."

"Press 'B' to fire."

"OK, that's another thing. You keep telling me to press all these buttons, but what am I supposed to do if I don't have a controller? I did have a controller, but it disappeared when I fell into your weird alien place! So now what?"

"Press 'B' to fire."

"YOU ARE THE LEAST HELPFUL PERSON EVER!"

"Press 'B' to fire. Like this." He held up his rifle and shot the cardboard cutout. His gun made a little "pew" sound and a tiny hole appeared in the cardboard. It looked like he had shot it with a pellet gun.

"Fine," I said as I felt around my gun for a button or

trigger. Nothing. "There's no 'B' button! Are you happy now? Can you take this…" At that moment, I squeezed my left hand (or where my left hand should be) and the blaster on my hand FIRED A GLOWING WHITE BALL! The white ball hit the cardboard and instantly vaporized it.

"WHAT WAS THAT?!"

"Very good. You might save us all yet."

Just then, a much larger, much scarier praying mantis cardboard popped up.

"Now hold 'B' to charge your blaster. When it gets to full blast…"

"THIS IS *FULL BLAST*? I'M INSIDE OF *FULL BLAST*?!"

Of course, Sergeant Sandpants wouldn't answer me. He just kept yapping away about charging and blasting and then other weapons that "you will discover along your journey." I attempted to leave at one point, but no matter how hard I tried, I couldn't seem to climb out of the firing range stall.

After a half hour, I vaporized a row of cardboard praying mantises with a machine gun and the sergeant deemed me ready to "defeat the alien scum."

"Oh nononono," I said. "Just point me to Eric Conrad, please."

A glowing vortex appeared behind me.

"You're being dispatched to the alien outpost in the Rocky Mountains."

"Nonononono…"

"Godspeed, soldier. Godspeed."

The vortex got bigger.

"NONONONONONONO!"

I tried running away, but it was too late. I got sucked in. *WHOOOOOOOOOOOSH!* Everything disappeared again. More skydiving milk snorting. Finally, the falling stopped. I kept my eyes closed for a second longer, praying that I'd open them to find myself back in Eric's basement. Bad news: no basement. Worse news: lots of snow. Worst news: a praying mantis the size of a tank was charging at me.

Saving Progress . . .
Do not close book while save icon is on the page

CHAPTER THREE
Blast Blast Squawk!

I did the thing you're supposed to do when a man-eating praying mantis starts charging at you. I screamed like a girl.

"AHHHHHHHH!"

The praying mantis did not slow down. I tried adding running to the mix.

"AHHHH…" Thud. "AHHHH…" Thud. "AHHHH…" Thud.

Running over snow-covered rocks with a blaster strapped to your arm is harder than it looks. With the creature almost on top o

me, I pulled out my last trick: screaming while curling into a tiny ball. But even that didn't work because the stupid blaster kept getting in the…

Oh. Wait. The blaster.

At the last second, I closed my eyes, reached up and

squeezed my left hand. The blaster recoiled, and I heard a shriek. I opened my eyes to see the praying mantis disappear into a ball of light.

Wow. I almost died. Inside of a video game. I imagined the funeral. "Here lies Jesse Rigsby of Middlefield, Ohio. He was tragically taken from us by a giant praying mantis while trying to save a video game world from fake aliens. He bravely led the resistance, which lasted for all of 10 seconds."

I looked around me. Snow and boulders everywhere, with a path leading deeper into the mountains ahead of me. No thanks. I turned and started walking back to find a way out of this mess. I got exactly five steps before…

CLUNK

I hit something and fell backward into the snow. Confused, I picked myself up and tried again.

CLUNK

I got up and inspected the spot further. It was open air, no different from anything else around me. I tried to put my fist through it.

CLUNK

Owwwwww! I punched an invisible brick wall. I shook my hand, then tried blasting it. Nothing. Maybe full blast? I charged the blaster and shot the invisible wall from two feet away. The ball of light absorbed into the wall and disappeared. I sighed, put my hand against the wall and started walking to find an opening.

After five minutes of walking along an invisible wall in the Rocky Mountains (not exactly an activity I thought I'd be doing when I woke up), I heard a noise to my left.

Clickclickclick.

I slowly turned. Through several pine trees, I could see two praying mantises scuttling back and forth, guarding the main path. Gulp. I slowed down and crept quieter to keep from alerting the…

CLUNK

The invisible wall had jutted in with no warning, and I clunked my head against it. One of the creatures turned. I stayed very still, because maybe praying mantis aliens are like T-Rexes, where they can only see things that move.

SQUAAAAWWWWWWWWWWWWWK!

Nope! Bad theory. Bad, bad, bad theory. The creature that had heard me was now standing on its back legs and making a creepy squawking noise, while the other one charged.

I ran as fast as my little legs would take me. While climbing over boulders and dodging trees, I kept reaching back and wildly blasting at my attackers.

Blast-blast-blast-SQUAWK!

Blast-blast-blast-SQUAWK!

It may not surprise you to learn that the creatures with six nimble insect legs were quickly gaining on the off-balance person who did not post a mile time to be proud of in gym class the previous week.

Blast-blast-blast-SQUAWK!

Blast-blast-blast-SHRIEEEEEEEEEEEEK!

Got one! Unfortunately, I had no time to celebrate because the mantis I had vaporized was replaced with another one who'd heard his battle cry. And then another.

I found the path and continued running and blasting wildly behind me, really wishing I'd brought my inhaler. But who brings an inhaler to a video game? I blamed Eric. He should have texted, "Come over. You're not going to believe this. Maybe bring your inhaler." Or perhaps, "Come over UNLESS YOU DON'T WANT TO GET CHASED BY MAN-EATING ALIENS THROUGH THE MOUNTAINS." You know, just to give me a choice.

As I ran and blasted, the terrain on either side of the path grew higher and higher until I found myself running through the bottom of a canyon. Praying mantises were now jumping into the canyon behind me, joining their brothers in a stampede of death. Suddenly, the canyon opened up into a big bowl with 50-foot walls. A dead end.

I ran to the end, turned around and started blasting. By this time, I was getting better at picking them off, but it was too late. For every alien I vaporized, three more would pour through the canyon opening. The horde got closer and closer. Thirty yards away. Then 20. Then just 15 feet. I continued shooting while closing my eyes, preparing to meet my end.

Then a chorus of shrieks. I opened my eyes to see the blinding light of five aliens getting vaporized at once. Before I could figure out what was happening, the wave behind them also disappeared.

"Jesse!"

I looked up. Eric. Eric Conrad, looking exactly like a superhero, was blasting away from the top of the cliff.

"Hey buddy! What do you think?"

"THIS IS THE WORST GET ME OUT OF HERE!" I screamed.

"Glad you're having fun! Try charging up to full blast!"

I did what he said. It worked! I got a whole group with one blast. Eric and I worked together on clearing the entire canyon of aliens.

After five minutes, the only group left was three stragglers coming in through the opening. I turned around to watch Eric line up the shot, and that's when I saw it. Sneaking up behind Eric was a jet black creature that looked a little more alien than praying mantis with five legs and one long blaster arm.

"Eric!"

He looked at me. The alien lowered its blaster.

"WATCH OU…"

The alien pulled the trigger, and my best friend in the whole world vaporized before my eyes.

CHAPTER FOUR
Reality Mode

Eric had been my best friend since first grade. The first time I saw him, his parents were unloading the moving truck, while Eric ran back and forth in the front yard wearing a coonskin cap and spinning the tail with his hand. I finally went over to ask him what he was doing. He said that he was trying to fly and was "getting close." I believed him because I was in first grade, and all first graders believe that they're *this close* to flying. I decided right then to stick with this strange flying child and learn his ways.

And for the next six years, I did stick with him. Through everything. We never learned how to fly, but we did learn how to jump pretty high off of homemade bike ramps and start fires with magnifying glasses and scare each other during backyard sleepovers until we were afraid to go into the house to pee. And now he was gone.

I blasted the alien that had blasted Eric, finished off

the group coming through the canyon, climbed up the rock wall to the spot where he'd been standing and sobbed the whole time. When I finally got to the top, I stood over the black spot where my best friend had been. There was nothing left. Nothing to remember my friend. What would I tell his parents? How would I even get back to his parents? I stared at the spot for a couple minutes longer, trying to wipe the tears from my eyes and forgetting that one of my hands was now a blaster and whacking myself in the face over and over and not caring.

"Whatcha looking at, buddy?"

I whipped around. "Eric?! What are you…I thought you…I saw…"

"Yeah, I got vaporized."

"THEN HOW ARE YOU HERE I DON'T UNDERSTAND HOLD ON ARE YOU A GHOST?!"

"No, dumb dumb. This is a video game. I just went back to the beginning of the level."

I gave him a weird look.

"Wait you thought I actually died?"

I continued my weird look.

"That would be crazy! That's not how video games work! You get killed once and you're done with the video game forever? Just throw it in the trash? No, you just go back to the beginning of the level and start again. It doesn't even hurt. See?"

Eric pointed his blaster at me. My eyes got wide.

"NONONONONONO!"

ZING

And just like that, I found myself back at the beginning of the level, staring down a charging praying mantis. One second later — *ZING* — Eric showed up too, and one second after that — *SHRIEK* — Eric blasted the alien.

"Come on," Eric said as he started walking down the path.

"Hey," I caught up to him. "You going to explain what this is all about?"

"Oh yeah!" Eric's eyes lit up. "Isn't this the greatest thing in the world? Can you believe it?"

"No! Definitely not! Is this real?"

Eric shrugged. "I think so. Earlier this afternoon, I finally beat the game. At the end of the credits, a screen came up that said I'd unlocked something called 'Reality Mode' and asked if I wanted to try it. When I said yes, I got sucked in like you did."

"But how did you text me?"

"Huh?"

"I asked how you texted me."

"Wait," Eric said as he dragged me into a small cave. "Watch this." He shot a small blast into the snow to get the aliens' attention. Soon, one came over, then two, then 50 or more. They were all trying to reach us, but they were all too big to fit into the tiny opening. Finally, Eric charged his blaster and vaporized the whole group in one shot. After the blinding light, we heard a chime and saw a mechanical part float over the snow. Eric *woohoo*ed, ran over and clipped it onto his blaster.

"Now I can launch grenades!" he shouted.

"Wonderful. Can you answer my question?"

"I don't think you're grasping the coolness of the situation here."

"And I don't think you're grasping that we are stuck IN A WORLD WITH ALIENS!"

"Oh, we're not stuck," Eric said as he started walking.

"Really?"

"Come on, I wouldn't have invited you in if there weren't a way out."

"So what happened?"

THUNK THUNK. I waited patiently while Eric shot grenades at two big trees. The grenades detonated in a flash of light, and the tops of the trees disappeared. Eric nodded approvingly.

"At the end of each level, there's a portal that takes you back to real life. I finished two levels, then decided to go back and tell you about it. I knew that nothing I could say would convince you to come in here because you're such a baby..." *THUNK THUNK.* Eric took out the alien that had shot him earlier. "...So I just had to let you discover it for yourself." He turned and smiled. "So what do you think?"

"I think this is horrible!"

Eric's face fell a little bit. "What?"

25

"What do you mean, 'what'! I have no idea what's going on, and…" Eric reached over my shoulder to blast a praying mantis running behind me. "…All of the sudden I get sucked into this thing and I think I threw up and you know how much I hate throwing up…" While maintaining eye contact, Eric held his hand out and launched a grenade at two aliens trying to sneak up on us to the left. "…And then this Army guy starts yelling at me and making me do all this weird stuff…"

"That was the tutorial," Eric interrupted.

"Huh?"

Eric held his blaster in the air and shot. A flying thing fell to the ground behind him.

"The tutorial. It's there to teach you how to play the game. That sergeant's not real — he's like a robot that's only programmed to do one thing."

"Whatever. And now everything's trying to kill us AND I HAVE MATH HOMEWORK THAT'S DUE ON MONDAY!"

"Listen," Eric said as he launched two more grenades just for fun. "I understand that you're a little annoyed right now."

"REAL ALIENS ARE TRYING TO EAT ME!"

"But you're with me, and I know this game backward and forward. If you stick close, I promise you'll be fine. Who knows, you might even have a little fun."

I glared at him.

"I'll let you shoot a grenade."

I glared some more. Eric unclipped his grenade launcher and put it on my arm. "Try it."

I squeezed. Two grenades *THUNK THUNK*ed out of my arm and vaporized a praying mantis that I didn't see sneaking up next to us.

"Wasn't that great?!" Eric exclaimed.

It was. It was very great.

"Hmf."

"Come on, we've got an alien base to defeat," Eric said as he ran ahead. Eric blasted and whooped his way through the rest of the level, and I launched grenades willy nilly. By the time we'd blasted our last alien, we were both out of breath.

This is it," Eric said, as he led me through a final door inside the alien base. Inside, we found a room with three glowing portals. One said "REPLAY," another said "HOME" and the last said "LEVEL 2."

"All right, I'll let you keep going," I said as I took a step toward the HOME portal.

"Wait." Eric grabbed me. "Don't you want to keep

going?"

"No. I told you I want to go home."

"One more level."

"Nope."

"The next one is in Hawaii."

"Sorry."

"They have jetpacks."

I squinted at him.

"Jetpaaaaaacks."

We stared at each other some more, Eric nodding and me squinting. Finally I rolled my eyes. "One more level."

"WOOHOO!"

We walked past the HOME portal into LEVEL 2.

It was the worst decision of my life.

Saving Progress . . .
Do not close book while save icon is on the page

CHAPTER FIVE
Jetpack Joyride

I probably don't need to tell you this, but jetpacks are amazing. This is something I learned firsthand when Eric led me to a spinning jetpack at the top of a waterfall right outside the portal. "Go ahead! Strap in!"

I strapped on the jetpack, trying hard not to act like this was the coolest moment of my life. "OK, now what?"

"Jump off."

"Excuse me?"

"Jump off the waterfall."

I looked over the edge. The bottom of the waterfall was at least 200 feet down.

"Nope. Nopity nopity nope. Can't I just launch from here?"

"You can, but it's more fun if you're falling first. Just press the button in your right hand to blast off and remember to land when it starts blinking."

Wait, when what starts blinking?"

"Exactly! Now go!" With that, Eric pushed me off the edge of the waterfall.

I've only tried the big diving board at the rec center pool once. Last year, Eric finally got me to climb to the top. At the top, I told him I changed my mind about jumping, so he "helped" by pushing me off. I landed on my stomach and got a red mark that lasted the whole day. The lifeguard kicked Eric out of the pool and I punched him in the stomach as hard as I could to show him what my landing felt like, but neither of those things stopped him from cackling about it for the rest of the week.

Now here we were again, me falling to a watery grave and Eric laughing above. If I ever survived, I would do a lot more than punch him in the stomach. As the river rushed toward me, I tried to remember what Eric had said. *Do I push this button? No, maybe this...*

WHOOOOOOOOSH!

The jetpack roared to life. I stopped falling, and for half a second I found myself suspended in midair. I noticed the impossibly green rainforest around me and the roaring river below and the ocean in the distance and thought that nothing could be more beautiful. Then I screamed into the air like an out-of-control bottle rocket.

"AHHHHHHH!"

I blew past Eric giving me a thumbs up at the top of the waterfall. "You got it!"

I certainly didn't have it. I was spinning wildly and super close to upchucking again. But after 30 seconds of doing a perfect impression of an untied balloon losing all its air, I finally started getting the hang of it. What followed was the best minute of my life as I flew around Hawaii by jetpack. *I flew around Hawaii by jetpack.* If there's a cooler sentence in the world, I can't think of it right now.

I was having so much fun *flying around Hawaii by jetpack* (sorry, just wanted to say it again) that I forgot about Eric's blinking warning. Then, 500 feet above a volcano, my jetpack started sputtering. I looked back. The fuel wasn't just running out, the jetpack itself was disappearing and reappearing on my back! I panicked and looked for a place to land, but it was too late — the jetpack disappeared for good.

"Oh no! Nooooooo!" I screamed as I fell toward the mouth of the volcano. I was so mad at Eric. Falling off of the 15-foot diving board is one thing. Falling into a pit of boiling lava is quite another. But just before I hit the lava, everything went white, and I found myself standing next to Eric on top of the waterfall again.

"Pretty cool, huh?"

"Would it kill you to tell me what happens when the jetpack starts blinking?!"

Eric laughed and strapped on the jetpack. "Come on!"

"Don't I get one?"

"Yeah, it'll reappear in five, four, three, two…"

Another jetpack magically reappeared in its place. I strapped it on, and we started flying. In the air, Eric explained the plot of this particular level. Something really stupid about the aliens using Pearl Harbor to launch their attacks and blah blah blah. I couldn't pay too much attention because I was *flying around Hawaii by jetpack*.

We landed on a secluded beach, found more jetpacks and took off again. When we got into the air, we were joined by two eagle-sized wasps. I nervously glanced over. One of them made eye contact and glared at me.

"What are those?" I yelled to Eric.

"Oh, those are dumb. Do this," he said as he looped high into the air, circled behind one of the wasps and blasted it.

"I don't think I can do that."

"It's not hard," Eric said. "All you have to do is…"

While Eric talked, the remaining wasp's eyes started glowing red.

"Eric, what is that?"

"Quick, pull up!"

I tried, but it was too late. The wasp zapped me with a laser.

"OUCH!"

Eric blasted the wasp and grabbed me. "Come on."

We landed on a black sand beach. At least I think the sand was black. It was hard to tell because everything was glowing red and pulsing. "Here you go, try this," Eric said as he led me to a suitcase with a Red Cross symbol on it.

I reached out to grab it. The instant I touched it, it disappeared in a flash of white and my vision cleared up. A warm tingle went through my body.

"Ooh, what was that?"

"Medical kit. Any time you get hurt, just find one, OK?"

"K."

"You ready to keep going?"

I smiled. "Let's do this."

Eric and I spent the day blasting our way through

Hawaii. We cleared out the enemy patrols on the beaches, collected new laser upgrades for our blasters and sunk all the spaceships at Pearl Harbor. At sunset, we landed on a cliff overlooking the ocean.

"See that island out there?" Eric asked.

I squinted. "Yeah, I think so."

"There's something really cool on it. You want to check it out?"

"What is it?"

But Eric had already strapped on a jetpack and jumped off the cliff. "You'll see!"

I sighed, waited five seconds and strapped on my own jetpack. "Wait up!"

I pushed to catch up with him, but Eric was about 50 feet ahead of me. Thirty seconds into our flight, the island still seemed a couple miles away. "I don't think we're gonna make it!" I yelled ahead.

Just then, a huge shadow fell over the ocean. Then — "SCREEEEEEEEECH!" I looked up to see a bat the size of a small airplane swoop over Eric and grab him with two massive claws.

"Eriiiiiiiic!"

At that moment, I felt claws dig into my own back.

CHAPTER SIX
Boss Battle

With me and Eric in their talons, the bats flew toward the tiny island. As we got closer, the speck of land came into focus — just a beach the size of a small backyard with a single palm tree in the middle. When we reached the island, the bats dive bombed, then — *WHUMP!* — dumped us onto the beach and soared off.

I brushed the sand out of my clothes. "Was that supposed to happen?"

"Of course!"

I walked toward Eric. "We have to talk." I put my finger in his chest. "You can't keep surprising me with…"

My voice trailed off, because as I talked a shadow fell over Eric. I slowly turned to see what it could be this time.

A sand monster. Of course. Why not.

Behind me, a monster made of sand rose from the

ground. It kept growing and growing — first the size of a one-story home, then two stories, then as tall as one of those old houses with a big attic on top. Its face formed into angry eyes and massive fangs.

I jabbed my thumb toward the furious monster behind me. "Wanna tell me what this is?"

"The boss!"

"I don't know what that means."

"This is a video game. Every few levels end with a big boss battle."

"You're speaking gibberish."

Eric rolled his eyes. "If you blast him enough times in a glowing spot on his back or on his belly, he'll disappear and the portals will pop up."

"Fine. I'll be happy to go home where people aren't constantly tricking me and pushing me off waterfalls!"

"Fine!"

"FINE!"

I marched in front of the sand monster, and it roared like a dinosaur.

"Ooh. Ooooooooh. I'm real scared." I said as I blasted it in the mouth. "What are you going to do, eat me?" I charged up to full blast and shot it in the belly. It fell over shrieking, then grew bigger and angrier.

"Go ahead! Eat me! It won't even hurt. I'll just come right back here, and we'll do the whole thing again, because this is a video game and video games are STUPID!"

"Oh shut up!" Eric yelled from across the level.

"What was that?!"

"Just save it. You know you're having fun."

"Oh really?! You know what would be fun?" I dodged a spiky sand ball that the monster threw at me. (It's sand, you might be saying. Sand is soft. How could a sand ball be spiky? I know, right? Video games are so dumb.) "What would be fun is having a real friend who explains things and lets me choose for myself!"

Eric blasted the monster in the back, and it fell over again. "What? So I'm not a real friend now!"

The monster grew so big that I couldn't see Eric any more, so I just started yelling at the monster's belly, hoping Eric could hear me on the other side.

"I don't know, real friends trust each other!"

I could hear Eric charging up his blaster. I charged mine too.

"Real friends know each other," Eric said. "And this friend knows that you never want to have fun or make decisions for yourself. So sometimes he has to push you a little bit."

"Well maybe you don't know me as well as you think you do!"

I blasted the monster's belly. Unbeknownst to me, Eric blasted its back at the same time. In slow motion, the monster looked at me, then turned around to look at Eric. Then a funny thing happened. Its head started twitching unnaturally. As the monster's head snapped from me to Eric and back again, it started to roar. Or at least, it started trying to roar.

"RO-RO-RO-RO-RO"

It sounded a lawn mower trying to start.

"RO-RO-RO-RO-RO"

Suddenly the sand monster and island disappeared. Everything faded away, and we were left in a bright blue room. On the wall, words started to appear as if they were being typed.

ERROR 2302. ACTIVATE HINDENBURG PROTOCOL?

- YES

- NO

"OK," I said to Eric. "What's the Hindenburg Protocol?"

His face was kind of white.

"I don't know."

"What do you mean you don't know?"

"I mean it's never done anything like this before."

"So should we pick no?"

"Yeah probably."

I walked to the wall and touched "NO."

The message disappeared. Eric and I looked at each other and waited for something to happen. Then the message started typing out again.

ERROR 2302. ACTIVATE HINDENBURG PROTOCOL?

- YES

- NO

"I guess we don't have a choice," Eric said.

He touched "YES," and the room faded away. The island and ocean came back, but no more monster.

"That was weird," I said.

"Yeah. Super weird."

Three portals started pushing through the ground in front of us.

Why don't we both get out of here," Eric said.

We walked toward the middle portal — the HOME

one — but stopped short once it began revealing itself. Something was wrong. The two other portals glowed bright blue and purple like before, but not the middle one.

The middle one was dull gray. And it was locked.

CHAPTER SEVEN
Mark Day

"What now?"

Eric backed up. "I...I don't know."

We're trapped?"

"I mean I'm sure there's a way out."

"Oh really?!" I blasted the locked door. Nothing. I chunked a grenade at it. Didn't even make a dent. Then I blasted Eric. He reappeared on the other side of the island. I started marching toward him. "This is all your fault!" I blasted him again. He disappeared and reappeared again. "Now what are we going to do?" Another blast. "Nobody knows we're in here!" BLAST. "And even if they did, what would they do, reprogram the game and erase us?" BLAST. "We're supposed to go on a field trip to the science center next week, and I really wanted to go to the science center!" BLAST. "This..." BLAST "...is..." BLAST "...all..." BLAST "...your..." BLAST "...fault!" BLAST BLAST.

By the end of my little speech, Eric was just hanging his head while I blasted him to video game death over and over again.

"I'm sorry," he finally said.

I glared and blasted him again.

"It is all my fault. I shouldn't have made you come without asking." He plopped onto the sand.

I sat down next to him. "No, you shouldn't have. But I did have a choice, and I decided to keep going. So I guess we're in this together."

Eric didn't say anything. He just kept his head down and started drawing a sad face in the sand. Except Eric is really bad at drawing, so the face looked like a melty pizza.

"Come on," I picked him up. "Let's find a way out of here."

We walked through the REPLAY portal and reappeared back on top of the waterfall at the beginning of the level.

"OK, I said. "When we got into the video game, it felt like we were falling, right? So maybe we just need to jetpack high enough to escape."

Eric shook his head. "Won't work. We'll bonk our heads on the ceiling first."

I looked up at the clear blue sky above me. "OK, Mr. Positive. What ceiling?"

"The whole world is way too big to put into a video game. So programmers make it look like their levels stretch on forever, but they put in these invisible walls and ceilings to keep you from leaving."

I remembered the invisible fence in the Rockies. "OK, but maybe there's a portal hidden somewhere."

Eric shrugged.

"Well grab a jetpack and let's see!"

We scoured every inch of our fake Hawaiian island. Eric was right - it was a lot smaller than I first thought. In a single afternoon, we had jetpacked over every acre of rainforest, trekked across every beach and even hiked up the volcano. No hidden portals. At Pearl Harbor, while we were looking for an unlocked spaceship we could use to escape, Eric spoke up.

"Do you think they'll have a Mark Day for us at school?"

Mark Whitman was a kid in our class who had disappeared last month. Word around town was that he had drowned trying to swim across the Mahoning River after a storm. Everyone pitched in to find him - they even brought in these special boats to look up and down the river. When they couldn't find his body after two weeks, they finally decided to hold a memorial service at school. They set up a gigantic picture of Mark on stage, and his big blue eyes stared at us while a bunch of people got up to say nice things about him. Then we got to go home early. I remember being sad, but also a little excited that we got an extra day off. I got mad at myself for feeling like that.

"Stop it," I told Eric. "That's not going to happen."

"I mean, you didn't tell your parents where you were going, did you?"

I was silent.

"And my parents were only going to be gone for an hour or two. They have no idea. How long have we been in here? Half a day? A whole day? They're probably already looking for us."

I knew he was right. My mom would probably think I'd gotten kidnapped, and my dad would say Eric and I were hiding in the woods. I glanced back at Eric. He looked like he was going to start crying. "Come on," I said. "Let's go back to Sand Monster Island."

We jumped off the cliff from before, jetpacked over the ocean and let the big bats take us to the island. Sure enough, the sand monster was back. We teamed up and defeated him in no time. This time, he didn't start glitching when we beat him. He just shrieked and disappeared into the island. In his place, the portals reappeared. But now instead of three, there were four.

"That's it!" I said, pointing to the fourth portal. "That's our way out!"

Eric shook his head. "No, that one just sends you back to previous levels." He took a closer look at the locked HOME portal. "Wait. Wait a second! Look at this!"

We ran to the HOME portal. It was still gray and locked, but over the lock was now written "LEVEL 20."

"What does that mean?" I asked.

Eric turned and smiled. "There are 20 levels in the game!"

"OK."

"Jesse, this door unlocks when we beat the game!"

Saving Progress . . .
Do not close book while save icon is on the page

CHAPTER EIGHT
Lady Liberty

I am not at all a huggy person, but I gave Eric the biggest bear hug of my life right there.

"Wooohooooo!"

It was an awkward hug because we clunked arm blasters, but neither of us cared. We ran through the LEVEL 3 portal and did the pitch black skydiving thing again. I must have been getting used to it, because I barely felt like puking this time. When we finally stopped falling, I looked up to see the Statue of Liberty towering over me.

"OK, tell me about this level."

"This is a good one!" Eric exclaimed. "See, all the aliens in New York City think they have you trapped on Liberty Island. Little do they know that the Resistance has turned the Statue of Liberty into a rocket ship! So you have to lure all the aliens into the Statue of Liberty, climb to the top, and escape by jetpack the second before Lady Liberty blasts the aliens to the moon!"

I stared at Eric with my mouth hanging open. Finally I said, "OK, I never want to hear you make fun of me for collecting baseball cards again, because that's the most ridiculous thing I've ever heard."

He kept grinning. "But it's cool, right?"

"It's cool that the Statue of Liberty is a rocket ship? No. That's dumb."

Eric shrugged. "To each his own."

"So how are we going to do this?"

"The problem is that there's only one jetpack at the top, and we won't have enough time to wait for a second one to come back before the Statue of Liberty blasts off."

"Wait," I interrupted. "Doesn't that sentence sound stupid? 'Before the Statue of Liberty blasts off?' I just feel like we need to stop for a second so you can admit how dumb all of this is."

Eric rolled his eyes. "So I'll run ahead of you and unlock all the doors. You wait five minutes, hit that alarm over there to attract the aliens and run like crazy up to the top with them chasing you. I'll be waiting there with the jetpack, and we'll fly off into the sunset together. Sound like a plan?"

"Yeah. I've always wanted to watch the Statue of Liberty fly to the moon with a bunch of aliens inside."

Eric grinned. "I know, right? Me too!"

With that, he ran into the statue and disappeared inside. After five minutes of counting, I pressed the big red button next to me helpfully labeled "ALARM."

BRRRAAAAAAANG

BRAAAAAAAAANG

BRAAAAAAAAANG

A loud alarm sounded, and the Statue of Liberty's eyes began glowing red in time with the noise. I didn't have to wait long for the aliens to show up. They started pouring onto the island from every direction. All kinds of aliens emerged from the water — some old friends like the praying mantises and wasps, along with some new ones, including these Transformer ripoffs and stretchy Slinky guys. I blasted as many as I could, then made a break for the Statue of Liberty when the number of aliens started to get overwhelming.

I had visited the Statue of Liberty a few years ago on a family vacation to New York, so I thought I knew what the inside would look like. As soon as I entered the lobby, though, I realized that the game developers had taken some, uh, "creative liberties." No more simple lobby and long, winding staircase. Instead, I found an elaborate series of platforms and ropes.

"Seriously?!" I shouted before climbing onto the first

platform. From there, I jumped onto the flame sculpture in the middle of the lobby, and then onto a third platform. I climbed a rope to the fourth ledge, then discovered a problem — my next platform was all the way on the other side of the statue. I considered climbing back down and looking for another way, but the aliens had already filled up the lobby below. In fact, they continued to pour through the door, steadily climbing on top of each other toward me. From above, the whole thing looked like rising water coming to swallow me. If I didn't move soon, I'd be alien meat. I reminded myself that I'd just reappear back at the beginning of the level if I fell into the pit of squirming, shrieking aliens, but it still felt super scary.

I took a deep breath and remembered something I learned during my training. "OK maggot," Sergeant Sandpants had said. "When you come across a large pit, shoot your blaster at the ground in the middle of the jump to give yourself an extra boost."

"WHAT ARE YOU TALKING ABOUT?!" I yelled at the time.

Now I knew. I took a deep breath, jumped as far as I could, then shot a blast down into the pit the second I started falling. It worked! The blast gave me just enough lift to make it to the other side. I continued climbing and jumping and blasting my way up the Statue of Liberty as the tide of aliens rose closer and closer to me.

In gym class, I've never been the best at pull-ups (and by "never the best" I mean "unable to do anything but hang from the bar like a noodle"), but I was able to climb up every ledge with no problem thanks to my new, strong mechanical blaster arm.

By the time I reached the top, I was actually starting to have fun. I opened a door and ran up the last staircase to the Statue of Liberty's crown. "All right Eric, let's blow this popsicle stand!" (I don't know where that came from. "Blow this popsicle stand" is something I have never said once in real life, but it seemed like something a cool video game hero might say.)

I stopped in my tracks when I rounded the corner. In the middle of the room was Eric, wearing a jetpack, pointing a blaster at me. Also, for some reason, he was wearing a gas mask.

Oh, and one more thing. His right arm was long, slimy and gray.

CHAPTER NINE
Bye Bye

Eric — or whatever that thing was in front of me — raised its right hand with five spindly fingers and started waving bye-bye. I was so confused that I barely noticed him aiming his blaster directly between my eyes. Then, just before he pulled the trigger, he got distracted. I followed his gaze. Next to me, in the shiny, metallic surface of the wall, I could make out the reflection of a hand sticking out of a box, waving wildly. Mr. Gas Mask adjusted his aim from me to the reflection and shot a red laser.

ZZZZZIIIIING

As soon as he shot, Eric jumped out of the box and ran at me. Gas Mask shot at Eric. Or at least, he tried to shoot at Eric. Instead, he shot Eric's reflection.

ZZZZZIIIIING

"WHOOOOMPF!" I wheezed as the real Eric hit me in the ribs and tackled me behind a box.

The thing pointed its blaster at us.

ZZZZZIIIIING

Eric blasted the window next to us. From the ground I could feel the first rumblings of a rocket taking off. I looked out the shattered window to see that we were moving.

"Come on!" Eric grunted as he jumped out of the window.

Before I could argue that this would be a lot better with jetpacks, the alien rolled left to get a clean shot at me. I took a deep breath, ran and jumped.

ZZZZZIIIIING

The good news was that the alien missed. The bad news was that I found myself plummeting to my death. Again. The Statue of Liberty rocketed past me, and I heard the screams of a thousand aliens discovering that they were getting a free ride to the moon. Then, just before everything disappeared in a flash of light, I saw a small speck wearing a jetpack fly from the Statue of Liberty's crown.

"Was that another one of your schemes where you don't tell me half the plan?" I yelled after we reappeared in the water off of Liberty Island.

Eric shook his head as he treaded water. "I don't know what that was. When I got to the top of the statue,

I heard something behind me. I thought it was you not following instructions, so I hid in a box to scare you. Instead, it was some weird alien wearing a gas mask."

"Wait, you've never seen that alien in this game before?"

"Never."

"That's creepy."

"Yeah. Super creepy. Anyways, it started poking around the room like it was looking for me, so I stayed hidden. Then when it couldn't find me, it strapped on the jetpack and waited for you. I figured our plan would work just as well without jetpacks, so I decided to stay hidden and warn you to jump out the window when you showed up."

"Wait, waving wildly from a box was supposed to be your way of telling me to jump out the window?"

"Of course. Wasn't it obvious?"

I squinted at him. "I'm sorry I don't know the hand signal for 'jump out of the Statue of Liberty.'"

"Well everything worked out just fine, didn't it?"

"Whatever, can we just get through this before any more creepy surprise aliens pop up?"

"Definitely."

We swam toward the shore of Liberty Island as fast

as possible. Because we are not the world's best athletes to begin with and because we had blasters strapped to our arms, it was possibly the slowest, splashiest, most pathetic swim the world had ever seen. When we finally reached the shore, we shook ourselves off and walked toward the glowing portals that had appeared in place of the Statue of Liberty.

Eric walked through the LEVEL 4 portal first.

WHOOSH!

Then I walked through.

WHOOSH!

Then, as I was falling through the blackness, I could have sworn I heard the faint sound of a third person entering the portal.

WHOOSH!

Saving Progress . . .
Do not close book while save icon is on the page

CHAPTER TEN
Captain Eric

"I'm driving!"

"Driving what?" I asked as I looked around to figure out where we'd landed this time.

Oh. Great. A swamp. A thick, smelly swamp. I picked up my right foot. *THHHHHHHWUUUUCK*. The worst. I was standing in six inches of muck, which meant I'd be walking in wet socks all day. I can handle snow, I can handle volcanoes, I can even handle house-sized sand monsters. I cannot handle wet socks.

"I'M DRIVING I CALLED IT!" Eric did not have wet socks, because he did not get teleported into the swamp. Instead he ended up on a future-y looking tank 10 feet away, and he was calling it at the top of his lungs.

"No way, that thing's going to get stuck in two seconds!"

"Not this tank!" Eric yelled. He disappeared into the machine, and five seconds later it roared to life.

VVVVVRAWWWWWWW!

The tank lifted a foot off the ground thanks to four small rockets on the bottom.

Eric popped his head back up. "Is this cool or what?!"

"Hey, I want to drive that!"

"Maybe you should have thought about that before I called it. You can shoot the cannon though! That's pretty cool."

I folded my arms across my chest. "Oh really."

58

Just then, Eric's eyes got huge. He grabbed the cannon, swiveled it around and blasted something right behind me. I turned around just in time to see a 20-foot crocodile alien that had been jumping out of the swamp disappear in a flash of light. I had to admit — it was pretty cool.

"You gonna jump on, or are you gonna get eaten?"

I rolled my eyes, sloshed over to the tank and climbed up.

"That's the spirit!" Eric said with a salute. "Now that you've boarded my vessel, I expect you to only refer to me as Captain Eric."

"Your vessel? I'd rather take my chances with the crocodiles."

"That's no way to talk to your superior, First Mate Jesse."

I turned the cannon around and blasted Eric. He vaporized and reappeared in the driver's seat.

Eric nodded. "Point taken." He then flicked a couple switches and grabbed the steering wheel. "Let's see what this thing can do!"

What it did was accelerate from 0 to 100 m.p.h. in a quarter of a second.

"AHHHHHH!" I said as my right arm, which had

been operating the cannon, nearly got ripped from its socket. I flew backward into the muck with a giant *SPLAT*. Now in addition to wet socks, I'd also be spending the day in wet underwear.

I climbed back on and pointed the cannon at Eric. "Watch it, captain."

He accelerated slower this time, but couldn't resist doing a donut once he found a clearing that was big enough. Then we took off through the level. After five frustrating minutes of trying to aim at aliens while Eric swerved back and forth, I realized why they don't let 12-year-olds drive cars and why they CERTAINLY don't let 12-year-olds drive tanks.

"Would you drive straight for one second!"

"I'm working on it!"

CRUNCH!

"And stop hitting trees!"

"I can either drive straight or I can avoid trees, but I can't do both!"

I sighed as yet another crocodile jumped out of the swamp and ate us whole. We reappeared at the beginning of the level for the fourth time.

"Get out," I said.

"No wait, I can…"

"Get out."

Eric huffed and swapped spots with me. I smiled. "Now that I'm driving, I expect you to refer to me as Captain Jesse."

He blasted me. After I reappeared, we set off. I was actually not much better at driving than Eric, but because he was so much better than me at shooting, we made it through the level in no time. Eric cheered every time he zapped an alien, and I whooped every time I got to use a fallen log as a ramp. I was having a blast. A Full Blast. If driving a car is even a little bit like driving a tank, adults should be way happier on the highway than they seem.

The trees overhead got thicker and thicker until we ended up in an enclosed swamp that was almost pitch black.

"What now?" I asked.

"This is the boss," Eric said.

"Are we supposed to be able to see him?"

"It's a crocodile with glowing eyes that light up everything when he emerges from the swamp."

"Terrific."

We waited in silence for a full minute. Nothing.

"Hey Eric."

"What?"

"Cool boss."

"He should have been here by now. He always shows up right away."

"Well maybe we needed to get like a key or something?"

Eric looked at me with scorn. "A *key*? What could a key possibly do to help us find a crocodile in the middle of a swamp? That doesn't even make sense."

"Oh, I'm sorry. I didn't know a game that turns the Statue of Liberty into a rocket ship is supposed to make sense."

"Whatever. I guess we can see if there's something we missed."

I turned the tank around and slowly started driving back through the dark swampland. That's when we heard it. A hissing noise up ahead.

sssssSSSSSSsssssss

"Is that something?" I asked.

"I don't know what that is."

sssssSSSSSssssseeeeeeeeee

"Shh, listen." It sounded almost like a hissing voice. Or actually, multiple hissing voices.

yyyyyessSSSSSssssseeeeeeee

"Yessee?" I turned to Eric. "Is that what they're saying?"

EEEEErrrrrrreeeeeeeeek

Caaaaaapan EEEEEEErreeeeeeeek

My stomach did a somersault. Captain Eric. Jesse. They were saying our names.

CHAPTER ELEVEN
Speed Run

Here's the complete list of things that are creepier than hearing aliens say your name in a dark swamp:

1. Nothing.

That's it. Nothing can ever be creepier than that.

yyyyyessSSSSSssssseeeeeeee.

EEEEErrrrrrrreeeeeeeeek.

yyyyyessSSSSSssssseeeeeeee.

EEEEErrrrrrrreeeeeeeeek.

Eric panicked and started blasting wildly ahead. It did no good. If anything, the voices only got louder.

yyyyyessSSSSSssssseeeeeeee.

EEEEErrrrrrrreeeeeeeeek.

yyyyyessSSSSSssssseeeeeeee.

EEEEErrrrrrrreeeeeeeeek.

I put the tank in reverse, and we started slowly

backing up. Both Eric and I remained silent as we drove back toward the boss area. Soon it was almost completely dark, and the voices sounded closer than ever.

yyyyyessSSSSSsssssseeeeeeee.

EEEEErrrrrrreeeeeeeeek.

I felt Eric's hand on my shoulder. I tried to comfort him. "I know, buddy. We're going to figure out a way out of here."

"But how?"

Eric's voice sounded far away. Not like he was lost in thought or something, but actually a couple feet farther than I remembered. I looked down at the hand on my shoulder. My eyes had started getting used to the dark, so I could just make out that this hand was bigger than expected.

"Eric?"

A face leaned in real close to me. An adult face. Making a "shh" motion with his finger to his mouth.

I did not shh. I did quite the opposite of shh-ing.

"AHHHHHHHHHHHH!"

Suddenly the voices stopped. Then two eyes from the swamp lit up. They illuminated our tank. They illuminated me and now Eric screaming like a chorus of small girls. They illuminated an angry man tearing me away from the steering wheel. They illuminated an army of aliens blocking our path out of the swamp. And they illuminated their leader — Mr. Gas Mask.

Our tank thief slammed the vehicle into drive and took off toward the army. The glowing crocodile ahead opened its mouth to swallow us whole.

"Hold on!" the man yelled back at me and Eric. A nanosecond before the crocodile could chomp down on us, the man pressed a series of buttons, and our entire tank did a barrel roll away from the mouth.

"You never told me we could do that!" I yelled to Eric.

"I never knew we could!"

Now that we had narrowly avoided the glowing crocodile, we found ourselves plowing through the army behind him.

"Don't shoot anything!" the man yelled back to us.

That seemed hard to do, since aliens were now grabbing onto the tank and trying to climb up. Before any of them could get too far, our driver found a log, used it as a ramp and hit the thrusters in midair to turn our tank into a flying missile. As we soared over the heads of our attackers, the driver did another barrel roll to shake the remaining aliens off our tank. We landed with a splash behind the alien army and tore back toward the beginning of the level with the aliens behind us.

While Eric and I had driven with all the grace of a dizzy cow, this man handled the swamp like he was born there. Every time a new crocodile jumped out of the water, he was ready with a zig or a zag or a flying barrel roll. Unfortunately, in addition to the new aliens jumping out of the water in front of us, the army behind us had regrouped and was gaining ground.

Just as the aliens started grabbing for the tank again, our driver jerked the steering wheel hard right, and we zipped down a small path that I hadn't noticed on our first run through the level. The path led us into a small dead-end swamp. We were trapped — our only hope would be to turn around and try jumping over the army again. But our driver was not interested in slowing. If anything he sped up. Directly into a rock.

"AHHHHHHHHHH!" Eric and I screamed as we closed our eyes and held each other, bracing for impact.

But we never hit the rock. Instead, we drove straight through it.

When we didn't explode into a giant fireball, I opened my eyes. We continued driving through blackness — complete blackness. I couldn't even see any kind of ground underneath us. The only thing I could make out was what looked like the bottom of a swamp *above* us. The man had driven us underneath the level.

After a few minutes, we popped back up. But we were no longer in swamp land. We emerged through a waterfall in Hawaii. Our driver didn't slow down. He drove straight into the ocean, went underneath the level again and popped out of the ivy-covered outfield wall at Wrigley Field in Chicago. We drove like crazy through secret passages in and out of more levels — the Golden Gate Bridge, the Nevada desert and the Atlantic City boardwalk.

Finally, at the bottom of the Grand Canyon, we slowed to a stop. For the first time since the aliens started talking, everything was totally silent. Our driver parked the tank and turned to say something to me and Eric. But before he could get a word out, Mr. Gas Mask jumped up behind him and grabbed his neck.

I raised my blaster. Our driver's eyes got huge. "DON'T SHOO…"

I shot.

Time literally slowed down. The alien dodged the blast by leaning backward almost in half. Then, just as the blast was going over his body, the alien lifted up one finger of one hand. The blast consumed his finger. Before we could understand what had just happened, time went back to normal and the alien stood up again. He looked at his hand, gave us a four-finger wave bye-bye and beamed himself into the sky.

Our driver, who'd fallen to the ground, stood back up and shook his head.

"You have no idea what you just did."

Saving Progress . . .
Do not close book while save icon is on the page

CHAPTER TWELVE
Source Code

The driver took us into a cave and parked the tank again.

"OK Jesse and Eric, what are you doing here?"

Eric threw up his hands. "How does everyone here know our names?!"

The man looked at him quizzically. "Well *I* know your names because I went to school with you."

"You don't look like any of our teachers."

"I wasn't a teacher. I was your classmate."

That's when I noticed the man's super-duper blue eyes. In my whole life, I'd only met one person with eyes that blue.

"Mark? Mark Whitman?"

He smiled a sad smile. "That's me."

Mark Whitman. I could kind of see it. You know those missing person posters that they age up 20 years to give you an idea of what the person might look like now? That's what Mark looked like, except the poster artist had also added lots of muscle and a blaster arm.

Eric was having a hard time keeping up. "But, but, but, but why aren't you drowned?"

Mark cocked his head. "Drowned?"

"Everyone thought you drowned in the river."

"Really? Who goes swimming after a storm?"

"Exactly!"

"No, I was playing *Full Blast* and got sucked in."

"Us too!"

"Yeah but why are you guys still young?"

We didn't know what to say. Finally, Eric spoke up. "Why are you old?"

"Because I've been in here for 20 years."

Eric nearly fell off the tank. "Whhat?! You've only been missing for a month!"

"What are you talking about?"

Eric and I filled Mark in on everything that had happened since he disappeared — the river search, the big photo of him in school, the Mark Day.

"So I got you guys a half day off of school?"

"Well yeah, but it wasn't a good half day because everyone was sad."

"And you're sure I've only been gone a month?"

We both nodded.

"That's great news! That means real time moves way slower than video game time. And if we're able to somehow find a way out of here, I can see my parents before they turn into grandparents!"

It was my turn to speak now. "What do you mean 'somehow find a way out of here'?"

Mark turned the tank back on. "I have something to show you."

We drove through a wall in the back of the cave. As we zigged and zagged through more levels, Mark explained that every video game has accidental shortcuts through unfinished walls and scenery. There are even gamers called "speed runners" who compete with each other to find these glitches and beat video games in record time. Over the years, Mark had found all of *Full Blast's* accidental shortcuts and made a home underneath the video game world where aliens couldn't reach him.

We eventually found ourselves back in the Nevada desert. We drove along the beginning of the level, hugging the force field boundary. Suddenly Mark snapped the wheel left, and we went through an invisible hole in the invisible wall. After driving through never-ending desert for 15 more minutes, we came upon a massive, black building. It looked kind of like a warehouse, except it stretched for miles.

Mark hopped off the tank. "Come on."

He grabbed the handle of a huge sliding door and creeeeaaaaaked it open. When we stepped through the door, lights automatically flickered a path in front of us. They illuminated row after row of filing cabinets and TV screens (the big tube kind) and abandoned metal parts.

"What's this?" I asked.

"The source code," Mark said as he led us forward. "All the files that make this game work are right here."

"Great!" Eric said. "Then we should be able to find one that we can use to get out of here, right?"

Mark shook his head. "I searched for a long time to find something I could use to CTL-ALT—DELETE my way out of here, but that's not the way it works. After years of digging and experimenting, I came to the conclusion that the only way out is through Level 20."

So what's the problem?" Eric asked. "I beat Level 20. It's not too bad."

Mark stopped at the end of a dead-end row. This particular section of the warehouse looked like it had been torn apart by someone desperate to find something.

The lights here flickered ominously. Files and pictures were taped haphazardly to the wall. There was even red yarn attaching everything together like in those police movies.

Mark pointed at the wall. "This is the problem."

At the top of the wall — above the files and pictures and red yarn — were two words scrawled in spray paint. Two words we had seen before.

"HINDENBURG PROTOCOL."

Underneath those words hung a familiar gas mask.

CHAPTER THIRTEEN
The Hindenburg Protocol

"What's, uh, what's the Hindenburg Protocol?" I asked while trying to follow the zig-zagging string.

Mark shook his head. "It's the thing that's going to make sure you never make it out of here alive."

Mark turned on one of the old TVs. The Hawaii level popped onto the screen. "When you were jetpacking around this level, did you notice the detail everywhere? Not just all the trees, but all the different types of trees. Sixty-seven to be exact. Sixty-seven different types of trees, each with thousands of leaves that all do something different in the wind. And did you notice the crickets? Not just the sound of crickets, but actual crickets and flies and mosquitoes zipping around. Do you know how hard it is to put that kind of detail into a video game?"

"Uh, hard?" Eric offered.

"Impossible," Mark said. "It's impossible to do that."

"Okayyy, so why…"

"It's impossible because even if you had enough time to code all of those different trees and bugs, you're creating infinite headaches for yourself. The more stuff you cram into a game, the more things can go wrong."

"Like glitches and errors," Eric said.

"Exactly. Every video game developer in the world is trying to make games that trick you into thinking they're more complicated than they are. Every developer except these guys. The *Full Blast* team has done the opposite because they built this." Mark tapped the gas mask on the wall and clicked a button on the TV.

The TV showed the beginning of the Hawaii level again, but this time, it zoomed in on a mosquito. The mosquito happily flew around, looking for someone to annoy. We watched the mosquito in silence for a full minute (which, in mosquito-watching time, is an eternity) before Mark spoke up.

"Notice anything weird?"

"Yeah," Eric said. "We're watching a mosquito on TV instead of trying to beat the game."

But then I saw something. "Ohhh wait, is it…"

It took a while to notice, but the mosquito was growing right in front of our eyes. It started slow, but as the seconds ticked by, it began growing faster and faster.

Soon, it was the size of a cat. After 10 more seconds, it reached human size. That's when the screen flashed blue and a figure appeared in the corner. Mark paused the video.

"Look familiar?"

It was our gas mask friend.

"That mosquito is a glitch in the game. I'm sure it started as a baby, and the developers forgot to put a limit on how big it could get. This is something that a human would usually have to fix, but not here. The *Full Blast* developers built their own clean-up crew. These guys. They're special agents called Hindenburgs."

Mark unpaused the video. Mr. Hindenburg Gas Mask scanned the mosquito with a laser thing and shot a net out of his blaster. The mosquito got tangled in the net, but it quickly grew too big and snapped the rope. Now it was the size of a tank. In a flash, the Hindenburg also got as big as a tank and shot a metal net at the mosquito. This time, it got tangled up for good.

Mark paused the video again. "The genius of the Hindenburg is its ability to learn. If it sees a mosquito getting bigger, it gets bigger too. When the mosquito snaps the net, it makes a metal net. It will do whatever it takes to destroy a glitch. With the Hindenburg Protocol, you can create the ultimate game, because you can build a world that builds itself. Any mistake gets zapped into oblivion, and only perfection remains."

"Great," I said. "So why is it trying to zap us?"

"You're the glitch."

"Excuse me?"

"Did you do something to break the game?"

"No, we were just fighting a boss."

"Both of you teamed up against a boss that only knows how to fight a single player."

We shrugged.

"So you broke the game, and now a Hindenburg is trying to make sure it never happens again."

"What did you do?" Eric asked.

Mark smiled. "I figured out how to ride those praying mantis things like horses. They don't like that too much."

"But you escaped your gas mask guy, right?"

Mark sighed. "I tried fighting him for years. But he's too fast. Too strong. Too smart. Every time I tried a new weapon on him, he'd dodge it, then learn about it, then create armor to protect himself from it. That's why I got so upset with you for shooting at your Hindenburg with the blaster, Jesse. Now we can never use a blaster on him again."

I looked down at the ground. "Sorry."

"It's OK, just know that you only have one shot with these guys. Anyways, my Hindenburg eventually figured out that I'm trying to leave through Level 20, so he's waiting for me there with thousands of aliens armored against every weapon in the game."

"I just don't get why they would put something like that in a game that sucks in real people," I said.

"That's the thing," Mark replied. "I've looked through this whole place, and there's not one mention of 'Reality Mode.' I don't think this game is supposed to suck in people."

"Then how are we here?"

"Someone must have added it after the game was finished."

"Who?"

Mark shrugged.

"One more question," Eric said. "What happens if the Hindenburg catches us? If he blasts us, we just go to the beginning of the level, right?"

Mark unpaused the mosquito video. The Hindenburg towed the tank-sized mosquito to the base of the Hawaiian volcano and pressed a small, smooth rock. The earth rumbled, the volcano sank into the ground and a giant pit appeared. The Hindenburg waited for all of the rumbling to stop, then rolled the mosquito over the edge into the pit. After 10 seconds or so, we heard the faraway thud of the mosquito hitting a metal bottom. Then the level flashed blue again and everything went back to normal.

"That's the Black Box," Mark said. "Even light cannot escape the Black Box."

Saving Progress . . .
Do not close book while save icon is on the page

CHAPTER FOURTEEN
High Noon

One shot.

According to Mark, that's all we had. The best way to make it count, he believed, would be to sneak up on the Hindenburg and use the most powerful weapons in the game at close range.

We spent the next hour raiding the warehouse for all the coolest gadgets we could find. Heat-seeking grenades? Check. Holograms? Check. Double-barreled bazookas? Double check. And everything conveniently fit into the handy-dandy tool belts Mark found for us.

Eventually, a plan formed. I would be the bait. Well not me, exactly, but a hologram of me. I'd be hiding in a safe place, while we'd project my hologram into the open to act as bait. When the Hindenburg would strike, Eric would trigger a cage to trap him and Mark would fly over with a jetpack to drop a giant bomb. Then we'd all swoop in and blast the cage with double-barreled bazookas, just to make sure that we got him and also because shooting double-barreled bazookas sounds really cool.

The plan seemed foolproof — none of us would get within 20 yards of the Hindenburg, and we'd blow him up before he'd have time to figure out what was happening. But something seemed off. As Mark ran through the plan one more time, I shared my hesitation.

"Guys, do you think this is the best idea?"

I do," Mark said. "I've given it a lot of thought over the years, and this is what I would do if I had to do it over again."

"I don't know," I said.

"Jesse just doesn't want to be the bait," Eric said.

I glared at him. "No, I just think…"

"It's OK widdle worm," Eric said in an annoying baby voice. "We'll make sure the big fish doesn't eat you widdle worrrrrrrm."

I turned to Mark. "Am I allowed to shoot him?"

"Definitely not. Are we ready to go?"

Eric saluted. "Aye aye, captain!"

I sighed. "Let's go."

We popped miniature radios into our ears so we could communicate from far away and hopped back into the tank. Mark drove through his underground shortcuts again until we reached the level where Mark thought our plan would work best — Hollywood. We emerged onto the set for what looked like a Western, cleared out the enemies and set our trap in front of the general store. I took a second to look at the ghost town, dirt road and bright sun. It was the perfect place for a showdown. I took my position in front of a green screen to film my hologram, Mark found a perch on top of the saloon and Eric finished the trap in the middle of the road.

When everything was set, Eric went into hiding and I flipped the switch to turn on the hologram. I didn't have to wait long for our friend to show up. When the sun reached its highest point in the sky, the Hindenburg appeared on the opposite side of the street. Showdown at high noon.

I held up my fists (well, one fist and one blaster arm) and nodded at him. He lowered his blaster at me and started walking closer. It was working. I danced in place, jabbing punches like some sort of prize fighter. He started walking faster, then running. When he was 10 feet away, he leaped into the air and pulled his fist back to do some sort of flying punch thing. Just as his punch was about to hit the hologram, I yelled.

"NOW!"

Eric sprung the trap.

CLANK!

A metal cage sprang out of the ground and trapped the Hindenburg. Instead of panicking, though, it calmly looked around for a few seconds before fixing its gaze on me. Not my hologram, but the actual building where I was filming. It slowly raised its four-finger hand and waved bye-bye.

"Guys, I don't like this," I said.

Mark was already in the air. "We got him!" he said over the radio.

The Hindenburg continued staring in my direction. It was almost as if he was expecting this. That's when I figured it out.

"ABORT MISSION!" I screamed over the radio.

He *was* expecting this. Mark kept flying.

"MARK! ABORT MISSION! HE KNOWS!"

The reflection. We had forgotten about the reflection. The first time we met the Hindenburg in the Statue of Liberty, we were able to escape because he got fooled by Eric's reflection in the metal wall.

"I've got him lined up," Mark said over the radio.

But you don't fool the Hindenburg with the same trick twice. And although a hologram isn't exactly the same as a mirror reflection, it's close enough for something as smart as the Hindenburg to figure out.

"Mark, stop this now!"

Mark dropped the bomb. The second before it landed, the Hindenburg disappeared. Or rather, the hologram of the Hindenburg disappeared.

BOOOOOOM!

The ground shook. Even as the dust from the blast was rolling through the street, Eric ran out of his hiding spot with his double-barreled bazooka.

"NOOO!" I yelled. I ran out of hiding to protect my friend. I reached the street just in time to see the real Hindenburg sneak up behind Eric.

"ERIC WATCH OUT!"

Eric looked at me with a puzzled look on his face. That was the last thing he did before...

BLAST!

The Hindenburg vaporized him.

"NOOO!"

BLAST!

In one smooth motion, the Hindenburg aimed into the air and vaporized Mark. Then he fixed his aim on me.

BLAST!

CHAPTER FIFTEEN
The Only Way

Not great. Not great at all.

After getting blasted, I joined Eric and Mark inside a bank vault at the beginning of the level, surrounded by alien guards. I tried shooting them.

BLAST! BLAST! BLASTBLASTBLAST!

"It's no good," Mark said. "They're all protected against our blasters now."

A praying mantis came over and poked us. It leaned in its weird alien head real close and sniffed before letting out a loud squawk and ripping off our utility belts. Then it left and the Hindenburg came in. He slowly walked around the vault, looking us up and down.

"Yyyyyeessssssseeeeeee," he hissed through the gas mask, looking at me. A shiver ran down my spine. "Kaaaaaapaaaaan Eeeeeerreeeeeek. Maaaaaaahhhhhhhk." He turned around and walked out of the safe. A moment later, we heard the sound of loud drilling.

"What's that?" I asked.

"If I had to guess," Mark said, "he's having them seal up the safe, and they're going to toss it into the Black Box with us inside."

Eric started to panic. "We've got to do something!"

Mark shrugged. "What can we do? All the weapons in the game are useless now."

That's when an idea hit me. Well, not really an idea, but maybe like 10 percent of an idea. "Not all the weapons."

"Yeah," Mark said. "All the weapons."

"*Almost* all the weapons. There may still be a way to escape yet. Eric, do you have any boogers?"

The look on Eric's face was a mixture of confusion that I would ask such a weird question and pride that he could produce giant boogers on demand. "Of course."

"Great," I said. "I have 10 percent of an idea."

Eric and Mark gathered around me while I whispered my plan. It felt weird to be the one coming up with the idea for once. Weird but cool. After I finished my plan, Mark stared at me with his mouth hanging open.

"I mean, we don't have to do it if you guys think it's a bad idea," I said.

"I think it's a crazy idea," Mark said.

"I know."

"I think it almost for sure won't work," he continued.

"I know."

"But it's our only chance." He put his hand on my shoulder. "Thanks for giving us a chance to see our families again."

I grinned.

"You've got good ideas, Jesse," Mark said. "Never be afraid to share them."

Eric was already digging in his nose for gold. "Got one!"

"Great!" I said as I moved behind the vault door with Mark. "OK, let's see what you've got!"

"WHOA, LOOK AT THIS!" Eric shouted with all the Hollywood skills he could muster. "I'VE NEVER SEEN ANYTHING LIKE IT!"

The drilling noises outside stopped. I motioned to Eric to keep going.

"WHAT DO YOU THINK IT MEANS?" By now, he was now holding the booger far away from his face and talking to it like he was in a Shakespeare play or something. "UH, WOW, IT'S SO BEAUTIFUL. IT'S

SOOOOOO BEAUTIFUL."

The vault door cracked open and a praying mantis peeked in. Eric didn't notice it because he was now in full acting mode. Mark and I squeezed farther behind the door.

"TO PICK OR NOT TO PICK, THAT IS THE QUESTION!"

The praying mantis opened the door wider and walked in. It was soon joined by two of its friends.

"A BOOGER BY ANY OTHER NAME WOULD SMELL AS SWEET!"

They got closer. And who could blame them? It *was* an impressive booger. All three aliens now had their backs to me and Mark. Just a few more steps…

"O BOOGER, BOOGER! WHEREFORE ART THOU BOOGER!"

"NOW!"

Mark and I jumped out of hiding and onto the backs of the two mantises closest to us. They squawked and tried to spin, but we grabbed onto their antennae. That was the key to riding them like horses, Mark had explained earlier — grabbing the antennae. When he saw us jump into action, Eric smashed the booger into the eye of the praying mantis closest to him, grabbed the antennae and spun around onto its back.

"Follow me!" Mark shouted.

We galloped out of the vault and past a horde of surprised aliens in the bank lobby. We almost hit the Hindenburg on our way out the door.

"This way!" Mark yelled as he turned left down the street. Aliens poured out of the bank behind us. We were on the set of a heist movie, and this was our car chase. We tore through the movie set while swarms of aliens flooded the streets behind us.

"Through here!" Mark shouted as we turned down an alley. The alley squeezed between two stone buildings and led us into the courtyard of a medieval movie. Without letting his praying mantis break stride, Mark grabbed a lance from a stand as he passed by. Eric and I followed his example. When we rounded the corner of a medieval stable, we almost ran into three fire-breathing aliens lumbering around the other side to meet us.

CLANG! CLANG! CLANG!

We sent them all to the ground with our lances.

Mark continued galloping toward the castle. He turned around and gave us a head nod to signal that we should follow his example. Unfortunately, his example was "gallop full speed at the deep moat." Mark pushed his praying mantis faster and faster as he neared the castle, until there was no chance he could stop before falling into the moat.

"MARK!" I shouted as his praying mantis went over the edge and Mark jumped off its back. He tucked into a ball and aimed for a spot in the moat wall. Sure enough, he'd found another shortcut. His body disappeared behind the wall.

Before I could reconsider following Mark's crazy cannonball maneuver, my praying mantis also jumped over the edge of the moat. I leapt off its back toward the spot where Mark disappeared, praying I had aimed correctly.

"OOF!"

It wasn't graceful, but I did it. One second later — "OOF!" — Eric joined us.

We ran in the darkness underneath the level until we came to a trap door.

"This is it," Mark said. "We're almost to the end of the level."

I couldn't believe that my plan was actually working! Just a couple more feet! My optimism lasted for all of 10 seconds until I cracked open the trap door. We were back on the Western set across the street from the glowing portals. But between us and the portals stood a massive alien army.

I closed the trap door. "They figured out that we

were coming here."

"How many are there?" Mark asked.

"I don't know, hundreds maybe?"

Eric sank to the ground. "Is there any other way to get to where we need to go besides the portals."

Mark shook his head. "That's it."

"So we're trapped underneath the level instead of a black box," Eric said with his head in his hands.

"No," Mark said. "No you're not." He walked to the trap door and cracked it open.

"What are you doing?" I asked.

"Getting you out of here."

"How are you…"

"After I jump out, I want you two to wait exactly three seconds before running like crazy to the portals," Mark said.

"Where will you meet us?"

Mark shook his head. "I'm not meeting you." He was starting to get emotional, but it was clear that he had already made up his mind. "Just please don't tell my parents. I don't want them to think I'm suffering."

"Mark, what are you talking about?" Eric stood up. "We're all leaving together."

"This is the only way," Mark said. "This was always the only way."

With that, he threw open the trap door and jumped out.

Saving Progress . . .
Do not close book while save icon is on the page

CHAPTER SIXTEEN
Back for More

I grabbed Mark's leg, but he was too fast and strong. Before I could say anything, he had already jumped out of the trap door and started to run away from the portals.

The aliens noticed him immediately.

"MARK!" Eric yelled.

Mark didn't slow down. He ran through a crowd of aliens directly to a jetpack.

"Come on," I said to Eric.

"But Mark…"

"Mark is doing this for us. Let's not ruin it."

By now, Mark had reached the jetpack, strapped it on and started to fly away. Before he could get too far, an alien grabbed him by the foot and tried dragging him back into the scrum. Mark pushed the jetpack harder, flopping in the air and blowing exhaust in the aliens' faces.

While Mark was singlehandedly giving the alien army all they could handle, Eric and I made a break for the portals. Mark's distraction only provided a slight opening, but that was all we needed. We were halfway across the street before the first alien stepped up. With no weapons to defeat the alien and no way around him, I tried the only other video game move I knew. I jumped on his head like Mario.

BOING! SQUAWK!

I didn't kill him, but I sure confused him. There was no time to celebrate, because before I had even landed, another alien showed up behind him.

BOING! SQUAWK!

And another.

BOING! SQUAWK!

Almost there! The last bit of road was completely clear until —

"HISSSSSSSSSS!"

The Hindenburg rolled in front of me, blocking the path to the next level. I sprinted at him screaming.

"AHHHHH!"

He reached out to grab me. Just before he could close his arms, however, I ducked and rolled. Much to his surprise, I wasn't going to the next level.

WHOOSH!

I rolled through the portal to the left — the one that led to all the previous levels. This time while I was falling, doors for previous levels rushed by. Eight, seven, six, five, four, three, two, one. I wasn't interested in any of them. Finally, I saw it.

TUTORIAL.

I grabbed the door and swung in.

Barracks. Sand. Sunshine. Everything was exactly as I had remembered it. Everything except the sergeant. Where was he?

"You back for more maggot?!"

There. Across the base. I ran to meet him.

"I need your gun."

"You can practice your skills any time at the firing range."

"I don't have time to explain! I just need your gun!"

After our failed ambush, the Hindenburg had learned about every weapon in the game. Every weapon, that is, except the one so basic that the game won't even let you use it — the sergeant's pea shooter.

"You can practice your skills any time at the firing

range."

Time had run out. An alien showed up in the portal.

I tried grabbing the gun from the sergeant. He had a vice grip, almost as if the gun were glued to his hands. Another alien appeared and then another and another and then the Hindenburg himself.

"You can practice your skills..."

Eric had been right. The sergeant was just a robot programmed to do one thing. The first alien through the door — a jumping lizard-looking thing — noticed us and started sprinting in our direction with windmill legs. I turned back to the sergeant and tried again to wrestle away the gun. When I turned around again, the alien was already in midair, just a few feet away. In one motion, I grabbed the sergeant and fell to the ground, using him as a shield.

As soon as the sergeant's pea shooter was pointed at the alien, he shot.

PING!

And his weapon, which to this point had done nothing more than poke holes in cardboard, vaporized the alien in an instant.

SQUAWK!

I turned the sergeant around.

"That was great! How did you know to do that?"

"You can practice your skills…"

Whatever. I picked him up by the legs and spun him around to face the oncoming alien army.

PING! PING! PING!

SQUAWK! SQUAWK! SQUAWK!

It was working! Kind of! The aliens were pouring in so fast that for every one that the sergeant vaporized, four more would take its place. I kept retreating with the sergeant until we found ourselves behind a big rock. The aliens closed in, chirping louder and louder with every step they took.

Then, silence.

I peeked around the corner of the rock. The aliens had parted ways, and the Hindenburg was approaching.

"Yesssssssseeeeeeeeeeeee."

I weighed my options. They were not great.

"Yesssssssseeeeeeeeeeeee."

If I stayed put, I'd be toast in 10 seconds.

"Yesssssssseeeeeeeeeeeee."

If I tried to take a shot with the sergeant, I'd be toast in five.

"Yessssssseeeeeeeeeeee."

If I made a break for the portal, the army would close in before I'd be able to take two steps.

"Yessssssseeeeeeeeeeee."

Maybe I could come out with my hands up and take my chances with the Black Box? I peeked out again to see the Hindenburg only five steps away. Then, just as I was going to take my first step out of hiding, I heard a faint sound.

WHOOSH!

Eric had finally made it through the portal. As soon as he appeared at the beginning of the level, he started waving his arms like a maniac. It took me a second to understand what he was trying to communicate, but when I figured it out — wow. *Eric, you big-boogered genius.* I ducked back behind the rock. I wasn't going to escape by going down in a blaze of glory or running away like a coward.

"Yessssssseeeeeeeeeeee."

I only had one option left.

BLAST!

I shot the sergeant.

CHAPTER SEVENTEEN
Final Battle

It was the fastest boss battle ever.

I'll try to describe everything slowly to make the battle seem longer than the 1.2 seconds it took. When I ducked behind the rock for the last time, the sergeant started talking again.

"You can practice your skills…"

I interrupted him. "I'm so sorry," I said before raising my arm cannon.

The sergeant, bless his little robot heart, did not react one bit.

"…any time at the firing…"

BLAST!

He vaporized and did exactly what Eric and I had been doing all game when we got shot — he reappeared at the beginning of the level. In Eric's waiting arms.

I peeked back around the rock. When he heard the

blast, the Hindenburg looked this way, then that way then finally behind him at Eric. Eric smiled and waved "bye-bye."

PEW!

The Hindenburg tried rolling out of the way, but he was too late — the sergeant landed a direct hit.

"wwwwwwwwhhhhhhhhaaaAAAAAAAAA…"

The Hindenburg looked up at the sky and let out an ear-piercing wail.

"…AAAAAAAAAWWWWWWWWWW…"

The wail built and built until it caused everything in the level to vibrate. Until it caused my insides to vibrate.

"…WWWWWWWW**RRRRRRRR**…"

I covered my ears. The rock in front of me cracked. The alien to my right popped — just exploded in a flash of light. Then another and another and pretty soon I was blinded by a sea of flashbulbs. The only thing I could see was the Hindenburg in front of me. Melting. I closed my eyes.

"…**RRRRRRAAAAAAAAAAAAAA!!!!!**"

The wailing reached its highest pitch, then faded away. I kept my eyes closed for a few seconds longer before daring to open them.

Carpet. Controller. Ratty, old couch. I was back in Eric's basement.

CHAPTER EIGHTEEN
Mr. Gregory

I found Eric on the ground next to me curled up in a ball.

"Hey buddy," I said. "We're back!"

He slowly opened his eyes and looked around the basement. Then he looked down. In his arms was a small toy soldier — a small toy soldier that looked exactly like the sergeant from the video game.

"What just happened?"

We looked up at the TV. The screen was black except for a single message:

HINDENBURG PROTOCOL ABORTED.

Eric pressed all the buttons on the controller, but the screen wouldn't go away. He restarted the game, but the message just came back. He even tried unplugging and replugging everything, but nothing worked. The game was fried.

Eric finally turned to me.

"Was that real?"

Of course it was real. Nothing had ever felt more real. And yet — the jetpacks, the grown-up Mark, the Statue of Liberty rocket ship — how could any of that have actually happened? We looked at the clock — 3:24 p.m. Not even one hour had passed since I'd entered the video game. The more Eric and I talked about all of our crazy experience, the more it felt like we had just woken up from a super weird nap.

We decided to visit the one person who could give us answers — Charlie's dad. We hopped on our bikes (it felt really sad to ride a bike again instead of a hover tank) and rode to Charlie's house. Charlie's family lived in the nice part of town in a home that looked kind of like it had been sent back from the future. Eric rang the doorbell.

Charlie came to the door and lit up when he saw us. "Hey guys! What's up!"

"Is your dad home?" I asked.

Charlie slouched. "Oh, uh, yeah. Sure. Wait here." He seemed sad that people were only using him to get to his dad again.

After a few minutes, Charlie's dad — Mr. Gregory — came to the door. He was a skinny man with big glasses and hair that looked like a porcupine with bed head.

"What can I do for you boys?" he said.

"You worked on *Full Blast*, right?" Eric asked.

"Sure did! How are you enjoying it?"

"Well," Eric paused and looked at me before continuing. "It tried to kill us, but other than that it was cool."

Mr. Gregory squinted at us and cocked his head. Eric went on to talk about everything that had happened to us that afternoon — Reality Mode and the Hindenburg and everything. At first Mr. Gregory looked genuinely puzzled. Then when we got to the part about Mark, he looked scared.

"That's impossible," he said when Eric finished. "You need to stop with these stories." Mr. Gregory may have been acting like he didn't believe us, but his pale face and shaky voice said otherwise.

"Please," I said. "You've got to believe us."

"I can't believe that."

"You've got to help us," I continued. "For Mark."

Mr. Gregory's face softened. "I promise you, I don't know anything. But," he glanced down the street and lowered his voice, "I'll see what I can find out."

107

"Thank you! Thank you so much."

That was two weeks ago. No one has seen Mr. Gregory since.

CHAPTER NINETEEN
Are You Sure?

"Yesssssssseeeeeeeeeeeee."

The Hindenburg got closer. I could feel his hot breath coming out of the gas mask. It reached one of its tentacle fingers out to touch me.

"Yesssssssseeeeeeeeeeeee."

I popped out of bed. Another bad dream — the fourth in the last week. Why couldn't I dream about flying around in a jetpack instead? Why did it have to only be the scary parts?

Eric and I had spent the two weeks since we escaped from the video game figuring out our next move. Where was Mr. Gregory? What could we do to save Mark? Who else could we tell? Did the whole thing even happen? In the meantime, Eric had sworn off video games — no need to take any chances. I, of course, did not need an excuse to stay away from video games for the rest of my life.

I lay down, closed my eyes and tried to fall back asleep.

"Jesse."

My eyes popped open again. I looked around the room. Nothing. But somebody definitely whispered my name, right? Or was this another dream?

"Jesse."

Out of the corner of my eye, I caught movement on the nightstand. I looked closer. Just my alarm clock, lamp, spelling bee trophy and sergeant action figure (I'd decided to keep the toy sergeant from the video game as a souvenir).

"Jesse."

It was the sergeant. The room was dark, but I definitely saw his mouth move. I got closer.

The sergeant took a stiff step forward.

"You can save him," he said.

"Save who?" I would usually be a little more hesitant about talking back to plastic toys, but I guess these things seem a little less weird after you've flown around Hawaii in a jetpack.

"Mark," he said. "But you have to go back now."

My head started spinning.

"Do you want to go back?"

"Yes," I whispered.

"Are you sure?"

SNEAK PEEK
Superhero for a Day

Continue Jesse and Eric's story in **Trapped in a Video Game Book Two**, *coming September 2016. To find out how you can get the first chapter for free before anyone else, visit dustinbradybooks.com.*

In the meantime, check out the first chapter of Dustin Brady's next book – **Superhero for a Day: The Magic Magic Eight Ball** *– due out August 2016.*

"There's nothing wrong with crying if it hurts."

"It doesn't hurt, so why would I cry?"

It did hurt. Very much. But Jared Foreman was determined not to show pain on video.

"Just a few more seconds. You can do it, buddy."

Kodey Kline, the kid behind the camera, was not Jared's buddy. Kodey was in sixth grade like Jared, but he had the chin hair of a high schooler. In James Ford

Rhodes Middle School, that was enough to make him a man among boys. Kodey mostly used his power to get people to do dumb things that he could then record and post online. He was the one who had challenged Jared to this particular feat of strength – attempting the splits while people stacked books in his arms.

"Five! Four! Three! Two! One!" Kodey led the small crowd surrounding Jared in a countdown. "Woohoo! You did it buddy!" He tussled Jared's hair and walked away.

"Hey!" Jared yelled. "Someone get these books!"

Although a few people stuck around to stare and snicker, nobody came to get the books. Finally, Jared had no choice but to tip over and let the books fall everywhere. He stood up, wiped himself off and started cleaning up. Another set of hands came to help him.

"Oh," Jared said when he noticed who the hands belonged to. "Hey Bre."

Breanna Burris was the coolest girl in sixth grade, or at least Jared thought so. She wasn't a "cool" cool girl – she didn't hang out with the popular crowd or take a million selfies or anything. But she was funny and athletic and always happy and, again, Jared just thought she was the coolest.

"You OK?" she asked.

"Oh, yeah. Yeah for sure." Jared said, trying to hide the fact that his face had started turning red. "Kodey just told me to - we thought it would be funny if I did the splits while holding a bunch of books. And it was funny! I mean, I haven't seen the video yet, but I think he's gonna put it up later..."

"Well I'm glad you're OK," Bre said with a smile as she picked up the last book. "Wouldn't want your pants splitting in half."

"Hahaha!" Jared overlaughed while she walked away. "No we wouldn't!" He smiled stupidly in her direction.

"You done fooling around?"

Jared spun around. His cousin, Lenny Patterson, was standing behind him with an impatient look on his face. Jared walked home from school with Lenny every day, and every day Lenny was late for some dumb reason. One day he would be trying to clean a giant ink stain from his pants, another the nurse would be testing him for a concussion after he had hit himself in the head with his own locker, another he would – well, you get the idea. Lenny would be fine waiting this one time.

"I wasn't fooling around."

"Yeah, you were too busy looking stupid for the Internet," Lenny said.

"No, it was funny."

"For everyone else. I don't know why you let him do that to you."

"Do what?" Jared asked. Kodey's a friend."

"Whatever that guy is, he is not your friend. Would a friend leave you with all those books?"

"He didn't hear me ask for help."

"And that thing last week, would a real friend dare you to eat a booger? Someone else's booger? And would a real friend trick you into calling the teacher "mom"? And would a real friend…"

Lenny spent the walk home recounting all the ways in the last month that Kodey had maybe not been a real friend. By the time they reached the park where they split off to their own houses, Jared had had enough.

"You're just jealous that Bre was hanging out with me."

Lenny squinted at him. "Just now? For like two seconds?"

"I would say ten to fifteen seconds."

"Because she felt sorry for you?"

"What? No! Come on. She thought it was funny too."

Lenny jumped and grabbed a branch above his head. He started swinging himself back and forth. "Whatever you've gotta tell yourself."

Jared didn't know why this conversation was making him so mad, but it was, so he did something to make himself feel better. He pushed Lenny. It wasn't that hard of a push – it shouldn't have done anything – but since Lenny was not the most coordinated of sixth graders and since Jared got him on the upswing, Lenny fell directly onto his back and got the wind knocked out of him. Since Lenny was on the tubbier side, the ground shook a little when he fell.

Jared crouched down to check on his cousin. "Are you OK? I'm really sorry, I didn't mean to do that."

This would usually be the time for Lenny to retaliate with a punch to the stomach. Instead, he lay staring at the tree he had just fallen from. "What's that?"

Jared followed his gaze to a small crevice in the base of the tree. Deep inside, tucked away so that it was only visible to someone lying on the ground, was something that looked round, black and plastic. Jared walked over and reached his hand in the hole until he felt it. Even though it was plastic, it gave him a small zap of static electricity when he touched it.

Jared pulled out the object and examined it. It was a black, oversized billiards eight ball with a small window on the back. Inside the window was a blue triangle that read, "DON'T COUNT ON IT."

"What's this?"

"You've never seen one of those before?" Lenny said as he sat up. "That's a magic eight ball."

"How does it work?"

"There's a dice thingy inside with different answers on every side. You ask a yes-or-no question, shake the ball real good, and the dice floats up to the window with your answer."

"Oh brother."

"See if it works. Ask it if Bre just 'hung out with you' because she felt sorry for you."

Jared rolled his eyes.

"Do it."

Jared sighed, held the magic eight ball to his mouth and asked, "Was Bre just feeling sorry for me?" He shook the ball, waited a second and got his answer.

YES, DEFINITELY

Lenny laughed as he turned toward his house. "Told you. See you tomorrow."

Jared stood glaring at the eight ball in his hands. "Why would she feel sorry for me? I don't believe you."

He sighed and started walking home. After a few seconds, he glanced back down and stopped dead in his tracks. The magic eight ball had a different message now. One that did not seem to answer a yes-or-no question. One that seemed very, very specific to his particular situation.

BECAUSE YOU LOOKED STUPID ON THE INTERNET

Read the rest of the story in Superhero for a Day: The Magic Magic Eight Ball – *due out August 2016.*

ABOUT THE AUTHOR
Dustin Brady

Dustin Brady lives in Cleveland, Ohio with his wife, Deserae, and puppy, Nugget. He has spent a good chunk of his life getting crushed over and over in *Super Smash Brothers* by his brother Jesse and friend Eric.

ABOUT THE ILLUSTRATOR
Jesse Brady

Jesse Brady is a professional illustrator and animator in Pensacola, Florida. If he got trapped in a Mega Man video game, he would totally dominate.

42476518R00073

Made in the USA
San Bernardino, CA
03 December 2016